You Good Fam?: An analysis of Mental Health in the Black Community

Copyright © 2018 by Gary Taylor

All rights reserved. No part of this publication may be reproduced, distributed, or transmitted in any form or by any means, including photocopying, recording, or other electronic or mechanical methods, without the prior written permission of the publisher, except in the case of brief quotations embodied in critical reviews and certain other noncommercial uses permitted by copyright law. For permission requests, write to the publisher, addressed "Attention: Permissions Coordinator," at the address below.

Lift Bridge Publishing
Info@liftbridgepublishing.com
www.liftbridgepublishing.com

Ordering Information: Quantity sales. Special discounts are available on quantity purchases by corporations, associations, and others. For details, contact the publisher at the email above. Orders by U.S. trade bookstores and wholesalers.

Please contact Lift Bridge Publishing:
Tel: (888) 774-9917
Printed in the United States of America
Publisher's Cataloging-in-Publication data

Taylor, Gary

ISBN 9781642546287

Chapters

Introduction

Mental Health vs Mental Illness

- Mental Health Defined

- Mental Health Statistics

- Major Depressive Disorder

- Anxiety Disorder

- Post-traumatic Stress Disorder

- Bi-Polar Disorder

Our Lense

African American Mental Health

- Why We Don't Seek Treatment

- Trust In The Medical Field

- Economic Disadvantages

- Cultural Competency

A Traumatic Past

- Slavery

- Jim Crow/Segregation Era

- Civil Rights Movement

- Police Brutality

- Mass Incarceration

- After Effects

- Substance Abuse: Alcohol

Suicide Prevention

Let's Get Personal

- Anger

- The Christian Perspective

- Learned Behavior History and Understanding

- The Family Dynamic

Just Pray it Away: The Black Church and Mental Health/ African-American Mental Health: Community/ Faith

- Depression in the Church

- Anxiety in the Church

- Dealing with the Mind in the Church

Closing

Resources

Acknowledgements

Dedication

I dedicate this book to my wife Shauniece M. Taylor and my daughter Aniah M. Taylor. I love you both and you guys are the reason I work so hard.

Excerpt

I am not sure about the first time I have really dealt with any type of mental health symptoms. If I had to guess, it would be around 2015 as it was the lowest moment in life. I never contemplated suicide, but I could feel the weight of the world resting upon my shoulders. I'm a Christian so in tough times I pray, but it didn't help. I would like to say I'm an optimistic person as well, however at this particular moment that didn't help. I couldn't shake this depressive episode. I am not sure if you ever sat there and just felt like you're in a fog; everything is present but you feel so detached from reality. You sit and watch life pass you by, you zone out, come back and repeat. You try to figure out what is happening and feelings of sadness, hopeless thoughts and emotions fill your mental. You ask when will it ever stop, when is it going to get better, when will I stop feeling the way I do? It was at that moment I realized how Depression can hold you captive, unable to express truly how you feel. Mental Health is real and it doesn't mean you are crazy. Additionally having a mental illness doesn't mean you are crazy either.

All Mental Health means is that you are human.

Introduction

If you're reading this book, you are on time. Get it? It's a Drake reference, play on words from his mixtape, "If You're Reading This It's Too Late? No? Ok cool, nevermind.

Greetings! My name is Gary T. Taylor, but you can call me Trey. I am the author and orator of this book. Throughout,I will attempt to examine why black people hate the words "Mental Health" and examine our history to find some answers. We will define Mental Health and Mental Illness, and become more familiar with the diagnosable illnesses. Now, I am not a doctor (as of right now just wait on it), but I do hold considerable experience in the field of mental health. I first obtained my Bachelor's of Psychology from Virginia Commonwealth University in 2011, and then went on to obtain my Masters of Social Work in George Mason University in 2015, with a focus in policy and advocacy. My work experience varies from non-profit work to for-profit work, employed by community agencies to working with hospitals and state agencies. Those settings include school, inpatient facilities and community settings. I have seen my fair share of Mental Health and I will share my thoughts on it throughout this book. So take this book as foundation to learn more about Mental Health. I am tasked to provide my community with education around this subject so we can address it properly. The education starts with the individual first. The individual has to be aware of their own thought patterns and behaviors and be willing to change them before anyone can help them. That's my ultimate goal to make you more aware. We often get intertwined with life making things more complex than they need be while neglecting that simple solutions can alleviate complex problems. Well this book is a simple solution in hopes of making black folks more aware of their Mental Health so we can start addressing it properly. Buckle up your seats, grab a cup of coffee or whatever you like and take a ride on this journey.

Mental Health vs Mental Illness

In this chapter, I wanted to provide an brief overview of data and statistics to show that Mental Health is real and is not something we just make up. Data sets from the Center of Disease Control and Prevention of Mental Health provides some pretty excellent numbers. These numbers continue to rise yearly and daily, some not even represented due to not disclosing or under-disclosing. We also see the definition of Mental Health and Mental Illness, terminology that often gets misconstrued in society.

According to the CDC (Center for Disease Control) and Prevention of Mental Health, Mental Health is defined as "a state of well-being in which the individual realizes his or her own abilities, can cope with the normal stressors of life, can work productively and fruitfully

CDC defines a Mental Illness as "collectively all diagnosable mental disorders or health conditions that are characterized by alterations in thinking, mood, or behavior (or some combinations thereof) associated with distress or impaired functioning.(www.cdc.gov/mentalhealth/basics). "

Now that you understand the difference between the two terms, remember this as you read throughout the book. I define Mental Health in the simplest way possible. Which is Mental Health, is how we deal with day to day life stressors.

Remember that as you read especially through looking back at our past in the book. Mental Health is synonymous with Physical Health, and Mental Illness or a Disorder is synonymous with a physical illness/medical condition. Keep that in mind as you read. Next we want to look at general statistics, along with some African-American general statistics.

- Approximately 1 in 5 adults in the U.S.—43.8 million, or 18.5%—experiences mental illness in a given year.

- Approximately 1 in 25 adults in the U.S.—9.8 million, or 4.0%—experiences a serious mental illness in a given year that substantially interferes with or limits one or more major life activities.

- Approximately 1 in 5 youth aged 13–18 (21.4%) experiences a severe mental disorder at some point during their life. For children aged 8–15, the estimate is 13%. (www.nami.org).

The general population statistics paint a broad picture of the reality of Mental Health in our country. The numbers at times may not look major, but considering that diagnosable Mental illnesses are on par with Medical conditions is becoming an increased issue. It shows that we as society deal with Mental Health more than we think. Let's examine below some statistics related to African-Americans and Mental Health. These are for those that reported, so understand these numbers could be higher.

- 63% of African-Americans believe that depression is a personal weakness. 56% believe that depression is a normal part of aging.

- 40% of African Americans report denial as a barrier to treatment for Depression

- 31% of African Americans report refusing help as a barrier to treatment for Depression

- 20% of African-Americans were uninsured prior to the Affordable Care Act

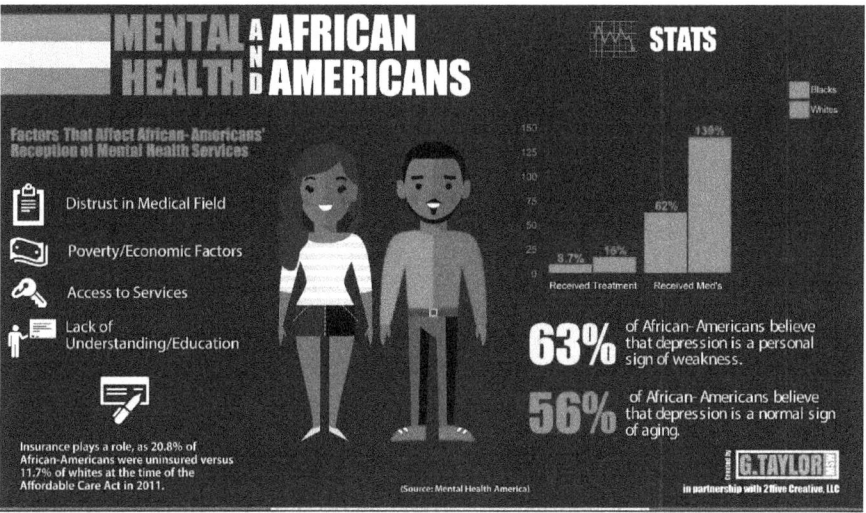

Here is an infographic me and the good folks at 21Five Creative, created to show why black people do not seek Mental Health treatment. It is a combination of date combined from earlier, and topics we will discuss later in the book. The barriers are plenty, but the hope is that after reading this book you will be more open to Mental Health, and not having fear when you need help.

Now that we have laid a foundation for Mental Health and Mental Illness, let's look at some of the more common illness you hear about. Those include Depression, Anxiety, Bi-Polar (everyone's favorite) and Post-traumatic Stress Disorder. All of these were pulled from NAMI's website (www.nami.org) or Mental Health America's website (www.mentalhealthamerica.net). Two of the biggest non-profits in the America that help reduce stigma around Mental Health, along with advocacy and provide great Mental Health resources to the community.

Mental Illnesses

Depression, Major Depressive Disorder

Defined as a mental illness that negatively affects how you feel, the way you think and how you act. It causes feelings of sadness and/or a loss of interest in activities once enjoyed.

Affecting about 26% of the population, 50% of those cases are linked to Suicide.

Signs and Symptoms

Helplessness, guilt, anger, social Isolation, withdrawing from family or friends, inability to concentrate, thoughts of dying, increased or decreased appetite, low energy, issues with sleep, irritability, increased alcohol or substance abuse.

Anxiety Disorder

Affecting about 18% of the population, defined as a

group of mental illnesses that cause people to feel excessively frightened, distressed, or uneasy during situations.

Types of Anxiety disorders

Generalized Anxiety Disorder- a severe chronic exaggerated worrying about events

Social Anxiety Disorder- intense fear of social situations that lead to difficulties with personal relationship, workplace or school

Emotional Symptoms: Feelings of apprehension and dread, feeling tense or jumpy, restlessness and irritability, anticipation of the worst or looking for signs of danger

Physical symptoms: Pounding or racing heart and shortness of breath, upset stomach, sweating, tremors and twitches, headaches, fatigue and insomnia

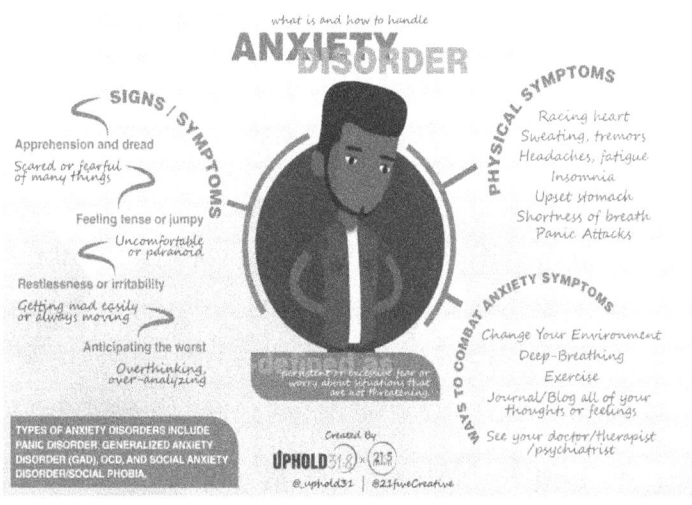

Post-Traumatic Stress Disorder

Post-traumatic Stress Disorder defined as an anxiety disorder that can occur following the experience or witnessing of a traumatic event. A traumatic event is a life-threatening event such as military combat, natural disasters, terrorists incidents, serious accidents, or physical or sexual assault or childhood. It affects over 14 million Americans, 4.4.% of the population. (Mental Health America)

Signs: Repeatedly thinking about the trauma, being constantly alert or on guard, avoiding reminders of the trauma

Symptoms: Panic attacks, physical symptoms, feelings of mistrust, problems in daily living, substance Abuse, relationship problems, depression, suicidal thoughts.

Bipolar Disorder

Affecting about 2.9% of the population, the average age of onset is around the age of 25. It is diagnosed as a chronic mental illness that causes dramatic shifts in a person's mood, energy and ability to think clearly.

Mania is described as an intense feeling or irritability or a feeling of euphoria. Hypomania is a milder form of mania where most can function. However mania the more severe form can lead to psychosis or delusions, mimicking schizophrenia.

Signs and Symptoms: Mood lability, irritability, lack of sleep, mania or hypomania, depression, excessive spending, large or outlandish ideas, pressured speech, bizarre behaviors or erratic

Now that you have a general understanding of mental health and some of the more common diagnoses, statistics, we can focus on the next series of areas specific to the black community. We'll first speak about those barriers to treatment and then we will look back into history. To understand why we believe the way we do we must examine the historical context and work our way back to present.

All definitions, signs and symptoms and treatment can be found at (mentalhealthamerica.net).

Our Lense

Before we jump into the barriers of treatment. I want us to understand a more personal experience when reading. A lot of the points in history I would categorize as traumatic and we have carried that trauma for generation. All of it isn't trauma but a mindset that makes us internalize our stress and emotions due to a traumatic past. Take for example "Big Mama" (everyone has had one right?). Stories exchanged about how many jobs she worked and how she took care of everyone in the family. Big Mama was a strong grandmother and would never sit down if you told her to. When Big Mama got sick, and her health started to fail, no one ever questioned her Mental Health. All of those days where she had to push and provide for her family, neglected her own physical and mental health finally has caught up to her. Maybe it already did, and she never told anyone. What we fail to realize is that improper care of our Mental Health has the same effects on our physical health. It can lead to the development of medical conditions or illness. Mental Health and physical anything go hand in hand. We continue to overlook those Mental Health symptoms and I am hoping after reading this book, you will take note of it.

 Let's examine psycho-social stressors for a minute, are you familiar with the term? Psycho-social stressors relate to the amount of social situations that affect us psychologically. Psychology is the study of human behavior. Our mental health capacity relates to how we deal with our day to day life stressors. In the realm of mental health we take psychosocial stressors into consideration when assessing for risk. It is an important part of the assessment that guides are clinical judgement. In this chapter we are directly speaking about social issues. The day to day psychosocial stressors include family, spouse/marital, parenting, legal, financial, employment, career, medical just to name a few, on a micro level. Look at the Macro level, systemic issues, whether it be housing related policies, discrimination, lack of representation in certain affluent levels, police brutality. We see these constructs and internalize these social issues daily, along with our own stressors and our mental health suffers out right. Maybe it doesn't manifest into a mental illness, maybe we ignore it and keep pushing on with our lives, maybe it manifests in our children down the line or their children, but it's there. If we do not address it now it will come up somewhere else in the future. It is almost biblical in nature, as the scripture says "What is done in the dark shall come to the light.". It's what makes us all unique and different. You got it? Breathe really quick and pause for a second take time to focus on the stressors you have in place. Are you properly addressing them? How is your mental health today?

As you can see Black Americans have been privy to tons of mental health issues, including numerous amounts of trauma. In our brief time here in the United States one could say we have experienced more trauma than any race currently in America. It guides the way we think, act and perceive life in America, all related to Mental Health. I hope this provided a different viewpoint of what Mental Health is. On to the barriers we face.

Why don't we seek treatment?

There are multiple reasons why African-Americans would not seek therapy. Look around, check out our history a lot can be said. With a history being disenfranchised, discriminated against or tested on like lab animals, it's not very hard to tell why blacks would feel a way about treatment. Below are some barriers that blacks face for receiving treatment for mental health. All will be discussed in details, in my observation of history of treatment. You have to think if we never liked going to a physical doctor then why would we do so for mental health or mental illness?

African-American Mental Health: Trust in the Medical Field

Black people don't like going to the doctor! It's true, I understand it and hear stories about it all of the time. Here I'm going to address, why we do not, and break down the lack of trust in the medical field. Rightfully so blacks have faced hardships since slavery. Once slavery was abolished, there was the Civil Rights Movement. Fast forward past Affirmative Action to 2016 you see blacks continue to face significant challenges.

Distrust in the medical field started way before any of us were even thought of. One of the biggest events that comes to mind affecting our trust in the medical field was the Tuskegee Study. This was when researchers wanted to study untreated syphilis in black men. Not to mention the men were not given informed consent, a commonplace practice of experiments of today. This experiment lasted for about 40 years. It killed a lot of black men, and ultimately was inhumane. That's just one example. However, oral stories passed down from generation to generation in the black community did not place such emphasis on going to the doctor. Home remedies, including a reliance on nature and other items proved to help us with the even most severe illnesses. It was that, along with the other injustices blacks faced through the medical field that made Big Mama and them to despise the doctor in my opinion. So, if physical health is such an issue for the black community then why would Mental Health be any different. According to the Office of Minority Health, 8.7% of adult blacks versus 16% of adult whites received treatment for mental health concerns in 2007-2008. 6.2% of adult blacks versus 13.9% of adult whites received medications for mental health concerns during 2008. Even more in a study found by Mental Health America, 63% of African-Americans believe that depression is a form of weakness. 56% believe it is a normal part of aging. Here lies a serious issue!

For us, as blacks, common diseases such as diabetes,

high blood pressure, cancer, heart disease runs rampant through our genetics. We are often being predisposed to those illnesses and the same can hold true for mental health. Spreading awareness about physical health but also mental health can help gain trust back in the medical field. Take for instance stress. Stress can cause many physiological concerns. It also is a key component in mental illnesses. If we look at how mental health affects physical health and vice versa, we can determine that to maintain a healthy lifestyle both should be examined. We cannot just neglect one or both and think we are living a healthy lifestyle. But we must erase everything we were taught about Mental Health and Physical Health to get to the place of acceptance and treatment. If not then our mindset will continue to be the same and nothing will change, and only get worse.

(Sources: Mental Health America, and Office of Minority Health)

African-American Mental Health: Economic Disadvantages

Access to services plays a huge role in why blacks do not take advantage of mental health care services. Again, the same topic can be equated to physical health practice as well. According to the APA, of the 34 million African Americans living in the United States, 22% of them live in poverty. That's about 7.5 million. That is a lot of individuals in poverty of which cannot afford access to mental health services. The Mental Health system itself is flawed and needs an overhaul; a topic for another day. Access to mental health services for anyone to see a therapist could be 3-4 weeks. To see a psychiatrist is about 6-8 weeks. The demand of individuals who are seeking treatment far outweighs the supply of mental health professionals evidenced by the waiting periods. Take for example, the black individual is seeking treatment. We have learned from the previous post that blacks have mistrust in the medical field, secondly to add, poverty plays a huge factor that the individual is facing. Poverty usually attributes to lack of healthcare coverage as well. There are places that offer services to individuals with no insurance. According to NAMI, 19% of blacks are uninsured. However, as the is reported the waitlist can be weeks out. Someone whose mental health is decompensating does not have time to wait to be seen by a therapist or two months to be prescribed medications (if they can afford them). Before a black individual even begins to seek services for mental health treatment they are already facing two barriers! Before entertaining the thought of treatment. That's not even the last barrier. Let's talk about cultural competency in the next post.

African-American Mental Health: Cultural Competency

In the social work field, we speak about cultural competency a lot. It's the fact that we work with such diverse populations in our field, it is important that we are aware of cultural values and beliefs before meeting with a client. Cultural competence can be loosely defined as a set of traditional values or beliefs belonging to a certain culture. America has their own culture in regards to manners, social norms, and traditions. Individuals from other cultures have a set of core values and beliefs that we often disregard when integrating into American society.

Often, African-Americans cultural values are stripped away automatically because we are "American". Technically that's not the case since blacks have their own set of cultural norms, beliefs and values passed down from multiple generations. I never understood why society chooses to disregard the black experience. However, in the realm of mental health there is a severe lack of mental health professionals. As if it is not bad enough that the number of clients outweigh the professionals; the lack of black therapists, psychiatrists, psychologists and social workers creates additional barriers. APA reports in 2011 only 2% of African-Americans account for psychologists. A report from NAMI shows 3.7% are members of the American Psychiatric Association, and only 1.5% are African-American. There is also a negative stigma in relation to lack of culturally competent mental health professionals in relation to treatment and services. The lack of the cultural competent mental health professional adds another barrier to blacks receiving service. It goes back to my first post; lack of trust in the medical profession. If I go to a doctor and they don't understand my culture than why should I go to that person? I can attest to multiple times where I can literally see the anxiety lift off the shoulders of my black clients. It makes them feel comfortable knowing that the mental health professional they are meeting is someone they can relate to. I am not sure how we promote more funding for more black mental health professionals. My job is not fun by any stretch but it is very rewarding. To teach reward over fun is increasingly difficult. I try to make it as creative as possible when I can in hopes of inspiring the black community to apply for more mental health careers. Here again it is not a "sexy" career, but it needs more black representation in the field to fulfill the demand of treatment but also to enhance diversity of black mental health professionals, so we can feel more comfortable.

A Traumatic Past

Black folks have never been excused from a struggle. If you examine American history, you can always point out where we have suffered. The problem is that we have never analyzed the mental health component of it all. Through this lense we can see trauma has been passed from generation to generation. Considering that only in the last 70-80 years we were treated as equal human beings. My goal is to not go extremely in-depth in regards to our social issues and history. The literature is abundant and supports the claims that will be made, and will provide proper historical context. The goal here is to examine how history has shaped our past, present and future. The goal is to provide an analysis from a Mental Health perspective on historical issues, hopefully can provide answers to why Mental Health is so taboo. It will also seek to answer why we think the way we do, and react as such. We can not dive deep into our social issues without looking at Slavery. The origins of slavery have roots in Africa, however the point of reference focuses on the Trans-Atlantic Slave Trade. This is where slaves were traded from African kingdoms to European settlers from the U.S. to South America and Caribbean islands.. No one knew the ramifications of what would happen once those Africans touched down in the New World, or as we call it the United States of America.

Historians also claim that Africans were bunched up in boats, often on top of one another, barely able to move. A tremendous amount of slaves during the slave trade, and even more became riddled with diseases, often dying before reaching their unwanted destinations. Slavery was one of the biggest genocides known to the United States. However, have you ever sat and thought about mental health played a tremendous role in it all. If you examine the horrific and if you would like to in more detail, again the literature is out there, especially at the African-American Museum both on paper and visually. Slaves were brought to the America, brought to a new and foreign place, they were torn away from their families and homes, introduced to new diseases, forced to work in harsh conditions, treated like animals, fed the leftovers of animals, raped, internal conflicts, slaves sold as property and traded, Willie Lynch Syndromes, beatings by whips and exposure to inhumane conditions. Nobody ever stopped to look at the mental health components of slavery? Not to mention how some slaves even when they became free, supposedly would not leave due to being conditioned to that way of life. At the time society knew nothing about Mental Health, and the terminology for Mental Health at the time meant "crazy." It is in this era, of so much vast trauma we see the molding of our ancestors. It is here where fight or flight, is a way of life for decades. The Mental Health of black folks, at this time exclusively was a constant state of stress and fear. Knowing what we know now, that can lead to a major illness, mental and physical. The perspectives from this time, gets passed down to the next generation, guiding their actions and reactions.

Jim Crow Era/Segregation

Fast forward after being set free and Lincoln abolishing slavery. I believe the Jim Crow Era along with Segregation paved the way for how black folks started to think and how they dealt with mental health issues. Again you see the generational mindsets continuing to be passed on from blacks and whites, especially from slavery. Jim-Crow era create and harbors the continuation of slave-owner mindsets. The rise of the KKK, also known as the Ku Klux Klan along with segregation proved to push the mental health of black folks in my opinion, to the edge. Imagine this slavery is over, traumatic in of itself. You are a Black American raising kids or have grown kids who now have to deal with the mistreatment due to the color of their skin, an issue you know all too well. The cycle continues, even though you thought it was abolished and over. Mental Health seems prominent and continues to peak during this moment, because there is constant feelings of being on edge. The fight or flight syndrome still is present and worse since you have children. The mistreatment daily due to being a brown person. You want to take about bullying? Brown versus Board of Education, remember that? The court case that found it illegal to keep white and brown kids separate in school systems? Could it be that even though the integration was helpful, did more harm than good? From a mental health perspective, think about it. You were once not allowed to share the same place as white folks which would often lead to violence, and racial slurs. Now, you are going to school as the schools with those same individuals. It's a catch 22, of which black folks deal with daily, that has affected their Mental Health since slavery.

Examine this for a minute, the case of Emmett Till. The teenager who was brutally murdered because he whistled at a white woman. The mother, Mammie had an open casket to show that racism exists in America and that it needs to be addressed. A similar tune right? About a year or so ago it came out that the white woman who reported that Emmett whistled at her, proved to not be true. Take a step back. We spoke about the Jim Crow Era and how it felt to be black during the time. Now, place yourself in the Mammie Till's shoes. Imagine after years of heartache, turmoil, maybe hatred towards this woman, friends and family grief. You find out that it was never true, that your son never whistled at the white woman, who told the police that he did.

Mentally that takes a toll, on an already strenuous mind. It's a hopeless place to be. It's place most blacks find themselves in, a helpless filled with frustration, anger, sadness, depression and many other symptoms. Yet we continue to believe that are current state of being, and perception is not rooted in a traumatic past.

Civil Rights Movement

Jim Crow Era led to the Civil Rights Movement, starting with the Montgomery Bus Boycott, paving the way for our beloved leaders Martin Luther King Jr, Malcolm X, and later

Medgar Evans, Fred Hampton, Bobby Seale and Huey P. Newton. The Civil Rights Movement was an important piece in history. Leading the pack, Martin Luther King set out to promote integration of all African-Americans into American culture, leading to the Civil Rights Act, which outlawed discrimination based on race, color and religion sex or national origin. Now we all know discrimination continues to happen in the United States in 2018, but this Act was very important for this Era, and future movements later. You're probably reading this and asking where does all of this fit with Mental Health. Consider the immense pressure of MLK and his journey. Tales of King on the road, fighting a battle for people of color, while either being supported or attempted to be killed. It's fascinating to think about and heart-breaking that we have never examined more about Dr.King's mental health during the movement. Did he ever think about giving up? I am sure. Did he ever have anxiety? I am sure. Did he ever become depressed or even suicidal? We don't know, but one could assume. If you sit and look at the multiple stressors in your life, then place yourself in Dr. Kings' shoes I am sure you could see the mental health symptoms one could have in that era. Non-violence itself is a practice of mental health in of itself...

You remember the teaching of sit-ins how they had to train those individuals to not react. Where they had to go through a simulation to of being berated, called out of their names. Their hair was grabbed and pulled, face slammed into their food. Their food may have been knocked off the counter. It was amazing and sad to witness. This was a training, a simulation of what to expect for sit-ins. A training that taught you how not to react or you would be harmed. It all relates back to Mental Health, and that training is the exact representation of black people in America for decades. The point that is missing in all of this, is the after effect. The rage or release, Mental Health symptoms that present itself years down the road or in other areas of our life subconsciously.

That era is a response to years of oppression of people of color. The movement had to take its toll on our grandparents, not just physically but mentally. All of the pent up emotions, fear, anger and rage mixed with anxiety, trauma, PTSD symptoms now has exploded into this either progressive non-violent movement or the "By Any Means Necessary" mantra. The latter seemed to continue on after the deaths of King and MLK. It led to the Black Power Movement. Groups such as NOI and The Black Panther Movement either were created or grew in power. You can examine history and see how these things are rooted in mental health as well over the deaths of our leaders and continue to deal with years of oppression. The trauma that we have faced as a people fueled these movements due to years of repressing our emotions and feelings.

Police Brutality

It's interesting to see the amount of issues black culture has faced in my brief 29 years of life. Look at the transatlantic slave trade to slavery, the Civil Rights Movement, Jim Crow Era and Segregation, Police Brutality, War on Drugs until present day. Currently the most prominent social issue that plagues the black community today is one that is nothing new to us,

Police brutality. Since 2014, there have been a series of killings of minorities by law enforcement, most notable cases Trayvon Martin and Mike Brown, plus many more. Those cases then shed a light into an ongoing issue in the black community, prompting debate worldwide. It is crazy to think how one's perception can skew their ability to reason, but we'll get to that later. I'm not here to re-visit who is wrong and right in those cases. I simply want to show how mental health plays a significant role in it all. As mentioned before police brutality is nothing new. The 90's birthed the LA riots after the beating of Rodney King, a black man who was pulled over and beaten. If you look back farther to the late 60's, you will see the creation of the Black Panthers, created by Bobby Seale and Huey P. Newton for self-defense.

Oral history passed down from generation to generation would suggest that "black folks do not like cops", end of story. Rightfully so, that has been the case for centuries, and every time we have begged society for justice for victims of police brutality we are met with resistance or claims that we are not being truthful; prompts intense debates.

I initially thought that in the Philando Castile verdict that it would be the turning point for police brutality cases, I was wrong. I thought it would be the case where future cases could piggy back from the verdict after all, there was video evidence. Not the case, I was heartbroken, as I was not sure what else could be done. With that said you can only help but wonder after all of the killings, lack of justice, and shared Facebook videos the effects of Mental Health on society, but primarily black people, let's examine. In the field of Mental Health, trauma is defined as "a disordered psychic or behavioral state resulting from severe mental or emotional stress or physical injury," (Webster's Dictionary, 2018). This means exposure to such experience has the potential to create Post- Traumatic Stress Disorder aka as PTSD, which we defined earlier in the book PTSD and trauma are not just reserved for veterans or medical conditions anymore. I'm of the mindset that we as human beings should not be exposed to death frequently.

Unless you are in that field that forces you to be comfortable with death, the average American citizen typically should not be exposed to such. Even in such fields, those workers still have to be sure to monitor their mental health along with secondary trauma. Examining the implications of the social construct police brutality in the black community, you have to be mindful of the trauma witnessed by survivors of the victim, the community, and also generationally. For example, Philando Castile case, we all witnessed the murder of Mr. Castile in his car in front of his child, and girlfriend. That video was on Facebook for public consumption. The result? The whole world privy to trauma. Increased fear, anxiety and agitation around law enforcement officials, whether that be them in uniform or a simple traffic stop. I was one, I understood and yet I work with law enforcement, but there is still anxiety and fear I feel when an officer pulls up behind me, this my friends is trauma, via increased mental health symptoms due a social issue black people have faced for centuries. No wonder we dislike and hate law enforcement so much. It's evident that the majority of every black person in America feels trepidation when it comes to law enforcement, a mindset, but also mental health component of Blacks in America.

. One could argue that African-Americans, have had PTSD ever since they were brought to America. The trauma again has just passed down from generation to generation.

Mass Incarceration

Moving along as promised, we have to take small look into mass incarceration. As stated previously, the amount of literature on the topic in the black community is prominent. Did you know that African American males make up of about 40% of the prison population, when we only encompass 14% of the US American population. These numbers are staggering for any persons of color however scholars have reported that this is the new slavery for Black Americans. In its creation, the prison system is supposed to be rehabilitative, we know it's not but it is supposed to. Incarceration affects the mind and mental health in a negative manner. I have worked with incarcerated men for about a year, and have spoken to those who are incarcerated to hear their perspective. Of my analysis their perspective of life has changed. Trying to change their way of thinking of incarcerated individuals takes a period of time. The freedom you once had outside is regulated to a correctional officer, that typically watches your every move. The judicial system once entered can be a vicious cycle that can be extremely difficult to get out of. Financial obligations, fines, fees, probation only piles up and can ultimately be the reason for those re-entering back into the system.

Mentally those incarcerated do experience a range of mental health symptoms. Once released they continue to go untreated, because the adaption of the mindset while incarcerated to internalize those symptoms. If anything, I can explain to you about mental health, is that it cannot be contained for too long. Mental Health symptoms show up in every facet of our life. For those incarcerated they are affected even more, because not receiving the necessary treatment while incarcerated, it continues on after release. Those symptoms also can be co-occurring meaning mixed with substance abuse issues. If you ask any previously incarcerated individual, they will tell you the worst place to detox from substances is jail. Match those with untreated mental health symptoms you have a whirlwind that can be extremely stressful to an individual coming home from the first time in years from incarceration.

The After-Effects

The detrimental effect we mainly talk about when speaking about the effects of mass incarceration is taking the male figure out of the household. Although African American women are five times more likely to be incarcerated, than white women a separate problem in of itself. I want to focus on removing the black male figure from the home, since it has been a trending topic of discussion for years. Focusing on the Mental Health of families of those incarcerated, we know one of the biggest issues of single-parent households affected by incarceration is finances. But what about the emotional and mental well-being of the children, spouse and other family members? One thing we know for certain, that a single-parent household is tough on children and the spouse, when both parents initially were present in the home. The spouse having to pick up the slack and the child who may not quite understand why their parent isn't home daily.

Focusing on the child, the detriment of mass incarceration may lead to children, teenagers acting out more often. The absence of a male figure in the home, could lead to disciplinary actions in school and engaging in behaviors that may lead to involvement with the judicial system as well. The emotional and mental health of the child is expanding as they grow, and trying to understand how to express their feelings and emotions could turn into anger, rage and resentment, all mental health symptoms. The perspective of the child could be skewed and ultimately develop a viewpoint of each parent that resents the both of them. I am only speaking from my experience in the field and what I have witnessed as a mental health professional. We only believe it's a mental health issue when it gets classified as a disorder, or diagnosable condition. I don't believe that it is an accurate way to address the issues of a child who has a parent that is incarcerated. Therapy is key here, in these stages or having an outlet to channel frustrations and emotions. Parental involvement in the therapy identifying and addressing thoughts about the incarceration, along with the emotions attached to it is instrumental in the child understanding the reason behind the parent-child relationship and reason for incarceration. At this level we are attacking the mental health component before it reaches a diagnosable condition. The same goes for the spouse and family members of those incarcerated individuals, except at this point we are dealing with adults. All the sentiments can be reiterated for spouse and adult family members of those incarcerated, but its heightened. The stress in regards to knowing a loved one is behind bars, not knowing what is going on or able to see them. The stress that comes with the financial burdens and trying to keep a household together that should be two instead of one. Their mental health can take a stark turn due to the multiple stressors that spouses and family members have to take on due to the fact. They too, warrant help and identification to treat their own mental health symptoms.

Substance Abuse: Alcohol

Switching gears from mass incarceration to reasons why some are incarcerated and expanding on co-occurring disorders; I want to examine substance abuse. Of course, we know there are multiple substances that have affected the black community, including the crack era and marijuana which both are driving factors in mass incarceration. But I would like to examine the detrimental effects of alcoholism, something that I feel in the black community is swept under the rug. I have lost two family members to alcoholism. I have seen it destroy families and individuals in its path. Alcohol by in large is a depressant, most use it in different consumption amounts for different reasons. Alcohol can lead to the increase of mental health symptoms. There are some that drink socially, and maintain moderation but others who drink excessively or binge drink. It becomes very dangerous when drinking daily, binge drinking or excessively. We should be aware of the amount of alcohol we are consuming. Are we drinking to deal with the stress of the day, are we drinking to hide our mental health symptoms? Are we dealing with unhappiness and other psychosocial stressors we may be dealing with? I have found through my career, and personal experience that we consume alcohol at high rates to suppress our thoughts and feelings. Keeping with the trend of how we in the black community don't acknowledge our mental health, we internalize those symptoms. One of the ways we do so, is to drink our problems away. Here lies where co-occurring disorders, chime in. The drinking of alcohol to cope or deal with life becomes problematic. Given the nature and severity of the trauma filled life we have had as black people in America I can understand why we would turn to drugs to cope. We have examined the many social constructs, and injustices we have faced since slavery. We have also examined that those generational issues, or traumas get passed down generation to generation and dispersed in multiple ways. If we are staying along those lines, then it makes sense because in that we have suppressed the our Mental Health symptoms along to use alcohol and any other substance that we favor.

Lack of coping skills, and avenues to get out what we are feeling and even not in our own circles for fear of being perceived as weak or abiding by this mindset that "you can not show emotions, because it shows weakness." has pushed us to find an outlet somewhere. Alcohol has the power to shut the body down, and destroy you. It has the worst withdrawal symptoms known to any drug. Before the opioid epidemic was rising, it has killed multiple individuals across the world either medically, or behind the wheel.

The numbers are consistent with the detrimental effects attached to it. I only want to highlight alcohol, because in the black community I do not feel we understand how and what we are drinking alcohol for. Once tolerable we have entered into a place where we can not function without it. Some need it to sleep at night, others need it to wind down for the day. What we fail to realize is that we have engaged in the use of alcohol to de-stress or deal with our problems and not develop healthy coping mechanisms. We are now rewiring our mind, and body to become dependent on alcohol in times of stress or any mental health symptom. If I am sad, I drink, I am happy I drink, I am grieving I drink. If I can't sleep I drink. If I am angry I drink. Understand it better. This is also the prototype for other substances as well. Alcohol is the only substance it seems that we do not look at as an issue in the black community, because again it has become normalized. Again, I am not speaking about those who drink in moderation and mindful of why and what they are drinking. I am no shape saying we drink more than any other ethnic group. I am simply talking about those who drink to suppress mental health symptoms, excessive drinkers, binge drinkers or those who have any idea why they are drinking in the first place. Understand it and address it no matter the age you are. The consequences could be stark.

Suicide Prevention

I debated about adding suicide to the book. Mainly because outside of Mental Health, we really do not like talking about it. Suicide is real though guys. Throughout the United States, Suicide is the 10th leading cause of death in America. That's right, it is Top 10! About 6.1% of suicides are African-Americans equating roughly to about actually know how to see but I'm now hearing that 2,750 blacks yearly. This is in succession with the other rates of death that we highlight in the black community.

What's more interesting is the rise of African American teenagers and suicidality. As the third leading cause of death for American teenagers collectively, between the ages of 15-24, young black teens seemed to be right in the middle of those rates, doubling or tripling for our black teenagers. It's scary, right? Well I am glad you picked up this book so we can talk about it more. The increase in bullying in our schools along with unrealistic pressures we face as a black community, internal and external has play a significant role. Needless to say Mental Health has been on the rise in the past decade as the economy and us as a people fight to stay on top of our lives. So let's talk about it. Suicide is the act of attempting to taking one's life. It could be done in a multitude of ways. There is also a difference between thoughts, plans, means and access. In the field these are some tools we utilize to assess suicidality. These also can become ways, where you the reader can identify these items, and hopefully get your loved one, friend or family some help. Ideations or thoughts we call them can be either passive or active in nature. Passive can be identified as thoughts of wanting to die, or not wanting to be here anymore etc. Active can be seen as thoughts that are immediate, filled with a plan, intention to do so and access to carry it out. One seems to be worse than the other right? Essentially you are correct, the latter although may involve a crisis and imminent danger. Both can have dire consequences, you ever hear about those deaths by suicide that no one seen coming? They tend to fall in line with the passive ideations. This means, that there were talks about it, nothing concrete leading up to ending their life.

Those are always interesting cases, because the signs do present themselves. Very rarely do signs of mental health crisis, regarding suicide not present. They can be small and range to large. They come in all forms. Some signs and symptoms, could be increased isolation, depression, anxiety, giving away their possessions, selling off their possessions, increased crying, sadness, hopeless, worthlessness, and so forth. The individual could stop acting like themselves or maybe over indulging in substance abuse like we spoke about earlier. Another one, is self-harm or cutting behaviors. Self-harm can include cutting on self, hitting self, using an eraser to scratch self and other tactics. Be careful with cutting, because often times those who cut are not suicidal. They tend to cut in order to feel a release, or maintain control when their mental health symptoms have increased. I would suggest if the concerns are present please take them in to be evaluated by a mental health professional. It's multiple nuances that we look over as a people. We have to get back to checking in with one another, having the ability to express our true feelings. Checking on one another doesn't mean that you are in someone's else business. It simply means that you care about that person and love them.

National Suicide Hotline:

1-800-273-8255

Text 741741 if you are in a crisis.

Let's Get Personal:

The next series of chapters outlines some more personal writings in relation to Mental Health in the Black community. These writings are from my blog where I either wrote out a series, or created a presentation to the community. The first falls right in line with Mental Health as we look into why are we so angry. After reading the earlier chapters you could see, where our anger would have built up from. Outside of that I go deeper into anger, something I have and continue to deal with personally. We all deal with it and it is a stigma that is attached to each and every one of us, but why? In the chapter I give a small glimpse into why our anger develops and can hinder us over time. The last piece is presentation that I have utilized multiple times at churches and at community events. A presentation that once started off as something strictly for churches has led to an introduction into Mental Health and Mental Illness. It also included scriptures to how we can utilize the bible with Mental Health .I called it Mined Over Matter, and I think it is important for anyone to witness if new to Mental Health. If you do not need the scriptures, cool. But the information provided is insightful. Of course it's a condensed version, as everything outline in this book, is mostly a part of Mined Over Matter. Let's take a look.

Anger

I wrote a small series on my blog talking about Anger. It was very personal to me, but I feel all black people would benefit from it. I outlined different perspectives, spiritual, social and family dynamic. At the time I was still struggling with my anger. Over time, I have grown to understand that a lot of black men and women to struggle with anger. But why? I try to make sense of it, through this chapter.

The analysis is taken from my experience and journey. Until recently I found how much Anger plays a part in our Mental Health.It almost is subsidiary of anxiety or fear. After all we do two things when we are feeling threatened, Fight or Flight.

This behavior chronicled by the human body is innate to us, denoted by the sympathetic nervous system, as the part of the nervous system that prepares the body for intense physical activity or fleeing from the situation. That adrenaline rush or feeling or super energy and power, yes the central nervous system creates it. Isn't the human body amazing?

Now some are constantly in the "fight or flight" mode categorized by individual who have post-traumatic stress disorder, or experiences some form of trauma in their life. I don't know about you but when I get angry i sometimes can black out. My heart rate increases, I feel light, I can feel myself ready to snap. My teenage years I would just snap yell, curse whatever prior to that in my childhood I would just fight. In my 20s and finding Christ, I tried so hard to change my anger. I did pretty well I think, actually a complete 360. I have a couple outbursts every now and then, but nowhere near the amount I had in my teenage years. Again it's a daily battle, and a lot of it is about control and letting go of things I've noticed. I also tend to believe it is a severe waste of time and energy. In my times where I became angry it has led to high blood pressure, and headaches. All of which affect our Mental Health. We neglect to even think about the role of Mental Health in all of this. I never came from a home that was surrounded in violence. People often equate negative households with negative outcomes. They never really see negative outcomes from positive or 'so-called positive households. You can receive bad ideals, or habits from positive households. Take the narcissistic individual who came from an affluent household, who grew up never understanding how to empathize with others, and ultimately being selfish in his ways. Did he grow up to being a great human being? No. Anger knows no class, race or color. Anger is our response to frustration, and is learned if not properly addressed at a young age. Anger can be built up emotion related to a trauma, or abuse. It can be related to how we see our parents, family members or peers react to certain situations. Anger is fluid.

Anger: The Christian Perspective

This is so self-explanatory any Christian should be able to write out this with no prompting. How does being a child of God equal up with dealing with anger? The Bible tell us,

"A hot-tempered person stirs up conflict, but the one who is patient calms a quarrel." Proverbs 15:18 NIV Man, a full sentence with such practical wisdom. As stated previously in earlier posts I struggle with anger daily. It has been one of my biggest hurdles to overcome, in my Christian walk. So many times, we react without thinking of how detrimental it can be. I'm sure Jesus had all the right in the world to be angry, yet he never once did. Whether it was the disciples denying him, Peter cutting ears off, or when he was on that cross and his own followers tortured and tormented him. He never once got angry, he only stated "father forgive them for they know not what they do." It's these words uttered by Jesus, that help us understand the type of love and compassion God has for us. It's only right that we do the same to one another. The bible also tells us that life and death is in the power of the tongue.

We also know that through anger we can often say things we do not mean. So, while angry you say something hurtful to the next person, they may take offense and never get over it, or the dynamics of your relationship may change. It would be so much easier, if while angry you say nothing until you have gained enough composure to vent out your frustrations appropriately. We tend to just explode, snap and go off. I understand I once did it too, matter fact I still fall short of this as well. The thing is that I am consciously making and effort to minimize my anger before it hurts me or another person. I encourage you to do the same as we are all striving to become more Christ-like. The other component is finding the source of your anger.

Anger: Learned Behavior History and Understanding

How does this apply to anger you may ask? I am a firm believer in behavior is learned. We are human beings and creatures of habit. To have a habit we have to learn it and feel some form of satisfaction behind or know there is a goal to achieve from it.

Considering anger, if we learn anger as a response mechanism to situations in life, we ultimately never learn how to appropriately respond to life curveballs.

This behavior can be learned from our household or family members. Linking the family dynamic to anger is important because it almost determines how you will react to situations in the future. If family members always yell when they argue about every situation, chances are you will do the same. If you never witnessed a disagreement over a topic in an appropriate manner, chances are you will not do the same in the future. If the only emotion you know how to respond with, in a situation is anger, then chances are you will always respond with anger.

Nonetheless, Behavior is learned but behavior can be unlearned, with a lot of hard work and dedication. It may take longer to change your emotional responses to situations, then it was to learn it. However, it is essentially a habit you must break, change and rebuild. Socially anger, never gets us anywhere. It is draining, makes us tired, and drains us mentally and physiologically. Learning how to replace anger with appropriate responses will not only break habits of learned behaviors, but ultimately makes us feel better as a human being in the long run.

Anger: Learned Behavior History

B.F. Skinner is one of the early philosophers who studied behavior, and introduced the concept of learned behavior and operant conditioning. Skinner used lab rats to show how humans learned through reinforcement and punishment, thus promoting the theory of operant conditioning. Positive reinforcement is shown by facing a challenge and receiving a reward once a solution is found. This is likened to the idea of a child, who is rewarded every time they score well on their homework assignments and receive a new game or toy.

Negative reinforcement is shown by taking away a reward if the challenge is not correctly done. In this case, if the child does not complete his homework, or receive good grades, the rewards such as games or toys will be decreased and taken away. This reinforcement reinforces supposedly positive behaviors.

The last is Punishment, which is not easily distinguishable between negative reinforcement. In this instance a punishment is something that is everlasting, and you remember continually. Touching a pot on the stove, and getting burned would be the result of punishment. Some researchers see spanking as a punishment that leads to adverse behaviors later in life.

Anger: The Family Dynamic

It's amazing how family influences the way you think and grow up to be. It is true you eventually do become your parents, and as much as young adults hate it, the process is inevitable. Household family dynamics can determine how you react to situations and determine how you behave later in life. It is one of the key ways you process your reactions. These things our learned throughout our life. When a problem arises as children we are always watching mother, father, sibling, or how another family member handles the problem. Is there a lot of arguing? Or does your family talk it out? Maybe your family sweeps things under the rug, minimizing the problem. Minimizing issues are even worse than anger and frustration because it lingers and builds up over time causing more stress.

What you were taught and witnessed as a kid in regards to emotions and reactions can ultimately determine how you react when faced with a problem. The mind is constantly learning and adapting to life situations. If all you have ever seen is anger or lack of compassion in your household and family; then ultimately it correlates to the same type of emotion and behavior later in life. So how do we break this cycle? Well one way is to identify how you respond to situations. Map it out. Describe the situation, write down the emotion attached to it, then write down your behavior also known as Cognitive Behavioral Therapy. Also, be more open with your family members and friends, once you gain up the strength to do so. It is important to break the cycle of anger in your family, by doing so you can save more than you know. Actively talking out your feelings with the ones who make you feel upset ultimately releases the anger into the air, and releasing control that it has over your life. Regardless if that individual even accepts or validates your feelings (50/50) chance they won't. At least it is still not on your heart.

The more you continue to attack and identify anger, and release it the easier it will come to control it over time. You'll also be an example to your family members in the future, your mental health and those around you mental health depends on it.

Just Pray it Away: The Black Church and Mental Health
African-American Mental Health: Community/Faith

I love God, I have faith in him that he can do all things. I honestly do not doubt in my mind, that I was created on this earth to do exactly what I am doing now. Community work, spreading his gospel, helping the youth and adults inspiring and motivating people. If we look through the bible some of the parables could be described as a mental illness. Whether it be David possibly in Psalms or was it Job whom God allowed suffering to increase his faithfulness to him. Remember the old terminology faith without works is dead? We used to say that a lot in my immediate circle. Faith is the substance of things we have not seen. We walk by faith and not by sight. If we have true faith, we understand that regardless of how it looks God will provide a way. The Lord provided gift to each human being. Career wise he chooses the paths of our careers before we even know it. MLK had faith enough to continue to fight in order of civil rights and integration between blacks and whites. He spelled it out in his I have a Dream speech. So here is where I believe the faith community lacks understanding about mental health. It is why it is so important in teaching and promoting awareness. If you are only telling a member of Christ whom is depressed, well just pray about it and God will make a way.

That is not enough. How are you supporting them in their time of need? Are you encouraging them to receive help? God created therapists, psychiatrists, and social workers for a reason. It goes beyond just prescribing medications, but it is about the support system an individual has in place. We can be Christian too, and have a special calling on our lives to counsel those who suffer from mental health issues. A prayer, an alter call in church is not enough to help an individual deal with their mental health. It's the precursor to the steps in faith that needs to be taken. To my church family please indulge yourself in learning more about mental health and understand how to better support your brother or sister in Christ.

As a result, I created a presentation called Mined Over Matter that was created to help introduce local churches to Mental Health, and also giving biblical principles on ways to combat mental health symptoms. A shortened version is listed in the next following paragraphs. It is not being served as a Intro to Mental Health for local community groups as well.

Depression in The Church

We defined Depression earlier in the chapters, and we now understand the signs and symptoms. We hopefully understand the illness much more and cannot realize that you just cannot pray it all away. Anyways, God also deals with depression too, certain characters in the bible can be categorized as either going through depression or showing what would be categorized as depressive symptoms. Names that come to mind our Job whom was being tested but lost everything he owned. One be depressed about doing good, and evil prevailing in life, for those we have a scripture for.

Psalms 34: 15-22, "The eyes of the Lord are on the righteous, and his ears are attentive to their cry; but the face of the Lord is against those who do evil, to blot out their name from the earth. The righteous cry out, and the Lord hears them; he delivers them from all their troubles. The Lord is close to the brokenhearted and saves those who are crushed in spirit. The righteous person may have many troubles, but the Lord delivers him from them all; he protects all his bones, not one of them will be broken. Evil will say the wicked; the foes of the righteous will be condemned. The Lord will rescue his servants; no one who takes refuge in him will be condemned."

Anxiety in The Church

Everyone knows the famous line when becoming a Christian, "wait on the lord" or the commandment that "worrying is a sin". But let's face it we are humans, and we worry or stress about things every day. Some things we worry more about than others, but in reality when you have a true certain faith in God you tend to worry less about frivolous matters and focus on the bigger picture at hand.

Understanding that God will supply all of your needs and make a way out of no way, can you tell I been in church for a while? Anyways, it's ok if we worry every once in a while because we are human and make mistakes. It's the constant worrying and lack of faith in God that become troublesome. Similar to the disorder, here are some scriptures that can help us with anxiety and our faith.

"Unless the Lord had been my help, My soul would soon have settled in silence. If I say, "My foot slips," Your mercy, O lord will hold me up. In the multitude of my anxieties within me, your comfort delights my soul." Psalm 94: 17-19

"Be anxious for nothing, but in everything by prayer

and supplication, with thanksgiving, let your requests be made known to God and the peace of God, which surpasses all understanding, will guard your hearts and minds through Christ Jesus." Philippians 4:6-7

"Let your conduct be without covetousness: be content with such things as you have. For he himself has said, "I will never leave you nor forsake you." So we boldly say: "The lord is my helper; I will not fear. What can man do to me." Hebrews 13:5-6

"But seek first the kingdom of God and his righteousness, and all these things shall be added to you. Therefore do not worry about tomorrow, for tomorrow will worry about its own things. Sufficient for the day its own trouble. " Matthew 6: 33-34

Dealing With The Mind In The Church

I placed the mind in this portion because I think it is important even though generic. When you become a Christian, and are baptized you are supposed to become a new creature, of new mind. In a sense, you are supposed to leave your past life, and begin your new life as a follower of Christ. Now some believe that this is an immediate transformation, and really it should feel that way. However, those old habits or your flesh do not fade away so easily. The difference becomes that instead of being by yourself you have a new support system, one of which that far exceeds man's understanding. Grace, mercy, forgiveness, repentance and prayer now are a support system in order to renew your mind, and change your old way of thinking and habits. The most famous scripture that comes to mind is

Romans 12:2 "And do not be conformed to this world, but be transformed by the renewing of your mind, that you may prove what is that good and acceptable and perfect will of God." So the reason why I use the Mind for this one is because biblically it speaks to changing the way you think, react and perceive things daily, an alternate version to our definition of Mental Health.

Here again, all things are related check out the scriptures below that deal with the mind.

"Finally, brethren, farewell. Become complete. Be of good comfort, be of one mind, live in peace; and the God of love and peace will be with you. " 2 Corinthians 13:11

"Examine me, O Lord, and prove me; Try my mind and my heart." Psalm 26:2 "Set your mind on things above, not on things on the earth." Colossians 3:2

"and be renewed in the spirit of your mind, and that you put on the new man which was created according to God, in true righteousness and holiness." Ephesians 4: 23-24

Closing

In closing, my goal of this book was to create dialogue around Mental Health in the Black community. I wanted to do a general overview of Mental Health in order to create a solid foundation of what it is. I then wanted to speak about topics dear to the Black community that we have dealt with for centuries. It is my hope that by reading the synopsis of those social issues and other topics that relate you would view it through a different lens. It is also my hope that you would look at your life in general and be able to identify your own Mental Health. By doing so, you could help another person, family member or friend. The more we understand about Mental Health, the more likely we are able to uproot traumatic experiences that continue to plague our community. I understand that we have overcome a multitude of traumatic incidents, and having to fight for equality for centuries. I do understand that a lot has changed for black people in America but also a lot has remained unchanged.

Whether that be racism, and continued discrimination or generational mindsets or perceptions of black people that we continue to push on one another. One worse than the other, but equally divisive to the Mental Health of the black community. As a result, there may be more books to come that can hopefully hone in on specific topics that plague our community. I hope this serves as an educational foundation and willingness to learn more about Mental Health, and continue to end stigma around it in the black community.

So tell me are "You Good Fam?"

Resources

NAMI (National Alliance on Mental Illness) www.nami.org

Mental Health America www.mentalhealthamerica.net

National Suicide Prevention Lifeline
1-800-273-8255

CRISIS TEXT Line
TEXT: 741741

Acknowlgements

First of all give all thanks and honor to God, my lord and savior Jesus Christ. That was churchy right? This book would not be possible if he did not give me the idea, and vision to write this book in such a short time. This book would not be possible had he not pushed me in the year 2016 to get this book out. Thank you Jesus

Thank you again to my wife and daughter for the constant daily motivation to get this book done. My wife for reading as I write, and supporting me among all my endeavors. I love you and appreciate you. My daughter, once you get old enough to understand that your daddy was an author!

To Lift Bridge Publishing for giving me the opportunity to release my first book. I thank you and love you guys. Ashley and Tony Logan are such inspirations and motivators I cannot thank them enough. You guys are sparking a new revolution of black authors and will be major contributors to black art in the future.

Special thanks to Tony Logan for constantly pushing me to write this book and just start it. My guy has been pushing me to write this book since 2014!! Brotha man you have been nothing but a blessing ever since we met. I appreciate you bro!

Thanks to the cover art designer my guy Chris Lewis. We grew up together basically, linked back up and it's been magic. Anytime I come and ask you to create something for me it's instantly amazing and you are able to make my vision come to fruition. Thank you bro.

To my editor Ryan Brown, I express much appreciation bro. We are pushing the culture forward when it comes to mental health. I am sure you cringed throughout the majority of these edits. Just know I appreciate you making me into a better writer and appreciate what you stand for!

To my DTP family, Kdot, Bazz, Dreez, Britt, and CJ. To the affiliates, Kenny, Brandon, AJ, Tim, Smash, Jermaine and my day ones Keem and Spizzy. I appreciate all of you guys, and all of the support you guys have given me over the years. Most of us got history dating back to 12 and 13 years old. Look at where we at now! Love yall man!

To my parents, the ones that raised me, birthed me and provided for me. I love you both Stacy Taylor and Stephanie Saunders. You guys do not understand the depth of the life lessons you have taught me over my entire life. I will ever be in-debited to you guys, and I am proud to call you my parents. You're son done wrote a whole book!!

Sit back and know your (Son) rise, sit back and know your (Son) set!!

CPSIA information can be obtained
at www.ICGtesting.com
Printed in the USA
BVHW04s2316030818
523344BV00007B/108/P